The Nature Detective Series

BUTTERFLIES AND MOTHS
Through the year

Allan Watson

D0434519

Illustrated by Richard Lewington
Series Editor Lionel Bender

Macdonald

This book was designed and produced
by The Oregon Press Ltd, Faraday House,
8-10 Charing Cross Road, London WC2H 0HG for
Macdonald & Co. (Publishers) Ltd, Maxwell House,
Worship Street, London EC2A 2EN

Series conceived, designed and edited by
Lionel Bender, 10 Chelmsford Square,
London NW10 3AR, assisted by Madeleine Bender

ISBN 0-356-09721-8

Printed and bound by William Collins Sons
& Co. Ltd, Glasgow

CONTENTS

Butterflies and Moths – Through the Year is designed to create an awareness of the butterflies and moths present in a garden, park, wood or open country, and indicate how they may be studied closely. Study may either be by direct observation of the caterpillar or larval stage feeding on a plant or the adult insect flying on the wing or resting on a flower or by the detection and interpretation of natural clues such as feeding signs or the clusters of eggs on a leaf. It can be used both in the field and at home as a reference book. The species included are mainly those likely to be commonly seen and readily identified in northwest Europe by a new nature detective, and the book is intended to give a grounding in identification and the searching for clues and evidence rather than providing comprehensive coverage of the many hundreds of different butterflies and moths and their signs it may be possible to see.

The book is split into several sections and is structured to lead from the search for general clues and evidence, which can be related to individual species, on to detailed practical study and project work. The information about the animals can be obtained without destroying their homes, surroundings and natural behaviour patterns since it is based on observation and not on collecting every item of relevance to identification. Using all the various sections of the book should give a more rounded view of butterfly and moth behaviour than would be obtained simply by catching and preserving the adult insects.

Body structure, pages 6-7
The various parts of the body of an adult butterfly and moth are compared and contrasted to help distinguish these two similar types of insect. Illustrations show all the body structures that are used in the identification key to adult butterflies and moths, pages 20-28.

Life history, pages 8-9
The cycle from egg through caterpillar (larva) and chrysalis (pupa) to adult is described. The shape and structure of each of the four stages in the insects' life history are illustrated, again to help in detective work.

Habits, pages 10-13
This deals with whether the butterfly or moth is active during the day or by night, what is the preferred food source of the caterpillar and adult, natural defence coloration or behaviour patterns that will help you in identification, mating behaviour and migration patterns.

Habitats, pages 14-15
Four major butterfly and moth habitats are described and illustrated. For each a checklist of the most common species of butterfly and moth is given.

Microhabitats, pages 16-19
Within a habitat there are many small, well-defined areas or microhabitats that are particularly attractive to certain butterflies and moths. Species that are always associated with particular plants or parts of plants are listed and discussed. A few butterflies and moths that are found in unusual microhabitats are also mentioned (some of these are not discussed in detail in the book but they are well-known species).

Observing, pages 20-21
Here are details of when, where and how to observe butterflies and moths.

Key to butterflies and moths, pages 22-28
A detailed, illustrated, comprehensive key to the adults of those species described in the Fact file section is set out to help identification of any specimens you may find.

Species fact files, pages 29-71
An introductory page explains the aims and structure of this the main section of the book and how it can be used both to help find and identify the various stages in the life cycle of butterflies and moths and to learn more about species that one perhaps already knows. Each page is presented as an identikit picture of each species discussed, with illustrations and descriptive text providing an in-depth and all-encompassing look at all the clues and pieces of evidence highlighted in the earlier sections of the book.

Practical section, pages 72-77
These pages look in detail at gardening for butterflies, rearing butterflies and moths and collecting specimens. They make suggestions for some nature detective work and will help to put into practice the theoretical contents of the book.

Areas to visit, page 78
A checklist of good sites to visit to observe butterflies and moths.

Useful addresses and further reading, page 79
This includes the address of some organizations which are able to provide further information to help with field study and details of books which supplement and extend the information in this book.

Index, page 80
A full index of the common names of species discussed in this book.

Parts of the body

The head of an adult moth or butterfly is the animal's sensory centre. It bears a brain, two large eyes, which can detect colours extending into the ultraviolet part of the spectrum, and a pair of antennae or feelers. The antennae not only feel but can sense smells, heat and movement and possibly infra-red radiation. There is also a mouth, connected in butterflies and most moths to a proboscis or tube that is coiled under the head when not being used for sucking up nectar and other liquids.

Behind the head is the thorax. This contains the large muscles that move the four wings. It also has three pairs of legs. In some moths there is a tympanum or ear on each side, and in most tiger-moths a sound-producing organ.

The wings, as in other insects, allow a freedom of movement rivalled only in birds and bats. Like the rest of the body the wings are covered with a layer of scales (flattened hairs). These scales not only improve the flying qualities of the wings but can be variously coloured to produce patterns that may help the two sexes of a species find one another, act as a warning to enemies or produce a camouflage effect.

The rear part of the body is the abdomen, which terminates in the mating organs in both sexes and the egg-laying organ in the female. One large group of moths has its pair of ears on the front part of the abdomen.

Differences between butterflies and moths

There are more similarities than differences, because these two groups of insects are closely related. However, it is not usually difficult to decide which is which at close quarters. Adult butterflies have clubbed (swollen at the tip) antennae whereas most moths have thread-like or branched antennae. Burnet moths, which have rather butterfly-like antennae, have the wings tent-like when at rest, unlike butterflies, which usually rest with the wings held together vertically over the back. The few other groups of moths with clubbed antennae are mainly tropical.

Although most butterflies are day-fliers and most moths night-fliers (nocturnal), watch out for day-flying moths.

Antennae

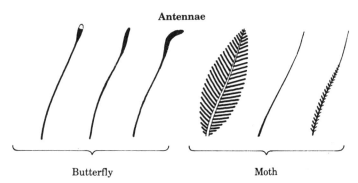

Butterfly   Moth

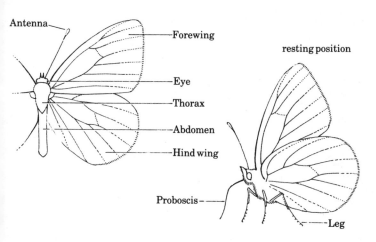

Antenna

Forewing

resting position

Eye

Thorax

Abdomen

Hind wing

Proboscis

Leg

Butterfly

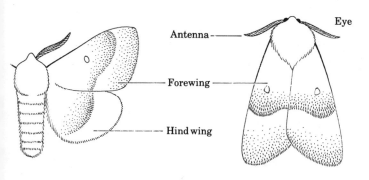

Eye

Antenna

Forewing

Hind wing

resting position

Moth

8   Clues and evidence ii – Life history

The sequence of life-history stages is always the same, but there are many variations in the timing. Some species complete more than one life-cycle each year, whereas others may take two years or more to complete one cycle.

Egg Eggs can be a variety of rounded shapes, from sausage-shaped to nearly spherical, or bottle-shaped as in pierid butterflies (whites and yellows). They can also be either smooth-shelled or ridged. Eggs are usually attached firmly to the foodplant but in some species they are scattered loosely over the plant (e.g. Ringlet and Silver-Y). They are laid singly, in batches, bands (e.g. Lackey) or strings (Map butterfly). The eggs of some species overwinter but most hatch into caterpillars within one to three weeks of laying. Sometimes the young larva develops inside the egg but does not emerge until after the winter (e.g. High Brown Fritillary).

Larva or caterpillar The larva's first meal is usually its shell, and from then onwards it feeds avidly, moulting its skin three or four times as it increases in size. Some species are gregarious, living together in a web or tent of silk spun by the larvae (e.g. Peacock and Browntail). Others live in a tubular shelter of silk or a rolled leaf (e.g. skippers) or make minute tunnels in leaves (small leaf-miners). A few tunnel into living wood (e.g. Goat and Leopard moths).

Larvae have groups of single-lensed eyes on the head, six thoracic legs with claws and ten or fewer claspers or false-legs on the abdomen. The body hair can be sparse, dense, or arranged in tufts. Some larvae have spines or horns. Many larvae feed for three to six weeks and then change into a pupa (chrysalis) but others overwinter before doing so. Some feed for two summers (e.g. Goat moth) before pupating.

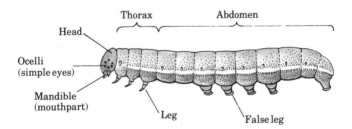

Pupa Most butterfly pupae are formed on or near the foodplant, most moth pupae either under the soil or on the foodplant. The pupa may be protected by a silk or partly silk cocoon made by the larva (most moths) or be unprotected (most butterflies). Transformation into the winged adult insect takes place inside the pupal case, the moth or butterfly eventually forcing its way out and at once inflating its wings until they harden. The pupal stage lasts for about two weeks except in those species that overwinter as pupae.

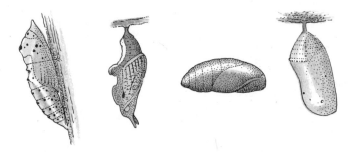

Adult The life-span of this stage is a few weeks – often from about two to five weeks – except for the few species that overwinter as adults, like the Brimstone and Small Tortoiseshell.

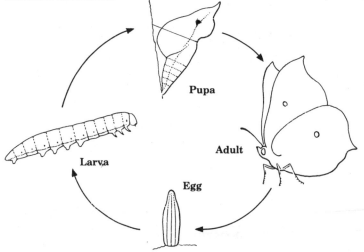

The life-history stages you are most likely to come across are the larva and adult. Each is active in different ways, at different times of the day or year and in different places, and provides good clues for the butterfly and moth detective. For example, a large hovering day-flying moth feeding from flowers in mid- and late summer is likely to be a Hummingbird Hawk-moth, while a small greyish-brown moth attracted to light in mid-winter will probably be a Winter-moth or one of its relatives.

Although nearly all adult butterflies are active only by day, not all moths are night-fliers. In Britain there are more day-flying moths than butterflies, although most of the day-fliers are small and not likely to be confused with butterflies. Watch out, however, for skipper butterflies, which have a fast wing-beat and are rather moth-like in flight.

Foodplants [See also Microhabitats, pages 16-19] Some knowledge of foodplants is very useful when you are searching for larvae or trying to identify them. In one group of butterflies, for example, the larvae feed only on the leaves of wild violets, in another group they feed on grasses; many feed almost exclusively on the leaves of trefoils and other pea-like plants. The larvae of some moths and a few butterflies are stem-borers or wood-borers. Many prefer cabbage-family plants, and others rose-family plants like wild strawberry. Some, like the British race of the Swallowtail, feed only on one species of plant.

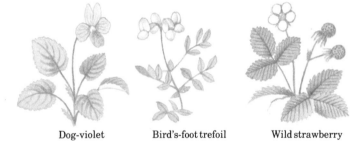

Dog-violet   Bird's-foot trefoil   Wild strawberry

The feeding habits of some adults is also characteristic. Few species except for some hawk-moths have a proboscis long enough to probe for nectar in long tubular flowers like honeysuckle. Important from the butterfly detective's point of view is the attractiveness of some flowers to numerous butterflies, even in large cities.

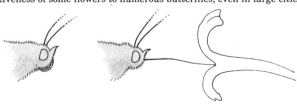

Defence Some of the defensive actions used by butterflies and moths make it easier for us to find them. Normally poisonous species like the Monarch butterfly, Cinnabar moth and burnet moths are brightly coloured to remind birds and other enemies that they are unpleasant to eat. The large eye-spots of the Emperor moth and the larva of the Elephant Hawk-moth probably frighten small birds but at the same time make the insect more conspicuous to us.

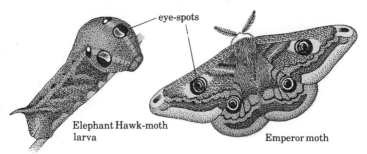

eye-spots

Elephant Hawk-moth larva

Emperor moth

Most moth larvae produce silk and some build large protective silken webs or nests on their foodplants. Web-makers include the Peacock butterfly and some of its relatives, the Browntail moth, Lackey and Processionary moths. Small silken tubes are constructed by many skipper butterfly larvae.

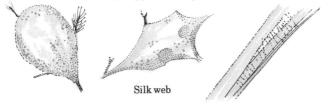

Silk web

Other defensive tactics and devices do not help the human or non-human searcher. Many adult moths and the larvae of some moths and butterflies hide away during the day and so avoid insect-eating birds, though not bats. Numerous resting moths match the colour of their background of bark, leaves or lichen almost perfectly, and the larvae of many moths and butterflies are equally well camouflaged. Clearwing moths and some tiger-moths closely resemble wasps, and deceive birds and other enemies as well as the human eye. Resemblance to some grotesque spider or giant ant is the speciality of the Lobster moth larvae.

Lobster moth larva

One of the best ways for butterflies and moths of avoiding enemies is to remain out of sight, as is performed by the larvae of leaf-mining, stem-boring and root-feeding species (e.g. the Turnip moth) or the larvae of the Pea moth and some blue butterflies that feed inside the pods of peas and pea-like plants.

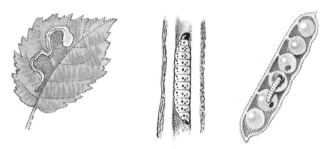

Mechanical methods of defence are shown by spiny and hairy larvae, which are usually avoided by most birds. Species like the Browntail and many tiger-moths often weave the irritant larval hairs into the cocoon surrounding the pupa. The female Browntail covers its eggs with hair from the end of its abdomen. The aggressive Puss-moth larva has a pair of filaments at the tail end that it pushes out and whirls around to ward off parasitic wasps and flies, mantids and other enemies.

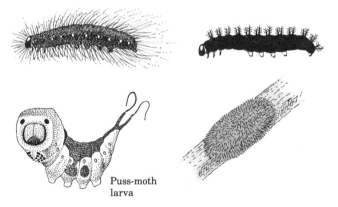

Puss-moth larva

Mating Adult moths and butterflies spend much of their time chasing, or being chased by, members of the opposite sex. The spiralling flights of many butterflies are often concerned with mating and each species may have a special ritual dance.

Colours are especially important to day-flying butterflies, which recognize members of the same species initially by the colour-pattern. Scents also play a part in mating. The male of many species have special scent-patches on the wings, or eversible (can be pushed outwards) scent-brushes or scent-tubes. Some females produce scents that can attract males, possibly from quite long distances.

Migration Migrations are long-distance movements in one direction, sometimes by large numbers of individuals. Butterflies such as the Red Admiral, Painted Lady and Clouded Yellow regularly cross the Channel during the summer, while the Camberwell Beauty occasionally crosses the North Sea to Britain from Scandinavia. British Monarch butterflies probably originate in the Canary Islands or Scilly Isles. The Silver-Y, Hummingbird Hawk-moth and several other moths are also regular visitors to Britain and northern Europe from warmer regions.

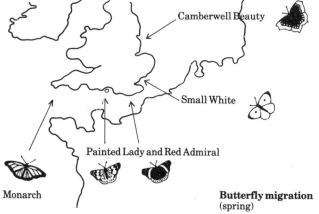

Camberwell Beauty

Small White

Painted Lady and Red Admiral

Monarch

Butterfly migration
(spring)

Each habitat has its special combination of species, usually dependent on the presence of larval foodplants. The Small Heath butterfly and a few others, however, can be found in more than one habitat.

Gardens and hedgerows

Gardens are one of the favourite habitats of the Small Tortoiseshell and Small White butterflies and the Garden Tiger-moth. You are also likely to see a Red Admiral, Peacock, Wall, Large White, Comma, and perhaps a Brimstone or an Orange-tip. Old hedgerows are the home of many species, including the Gatekeeper, Green-veined White, Orange-tip and many moths. You can also expect to see a Speckled Wood and possibly a Green Hairstreak if there are large trees along the hedge.

Meadows and Chalk-downs

The flowers and long grass of meadows attract various skippers, the Small Heath, Clouded Yellow, Meadow Brown and Common Blue butterflies and several grass-feeding moths. On grassy chalkhills in S. England you are likely to spot such species as the Chalk-hill, Little and Adonis Blues, Silver-spotted Skipper and Marbled White.

Woodland

Woodlands, of oak and other deciduous trees in England or a mixture of deciduous and coniferous trees in Scotland, provide a home for several kinds of butterflies and moths. Woodland specialists include the Wood White, several fritillaries, the Ringlet, Speckled Wood, Purple Emperor, White Admiral, Large Tortoiseshell, Chequered Skipper and most of the hairstreaks.

Heaths and bogs

Sandy heaths are the habitat of the Silver-studded Blue, but you are also likely to see Brimstones, Holly Blues, Small Coppers, Small Heaths, Graylings and other butterflies. Heathland moths include the Bilberry Pug, Common Heath, Emperor and Fox moths. The typical plants are heather (*Calluna*), heaths (*Erica*), gorse and bilberry. Peat bogs, usually covered with sphagnum moss and edged with sedges and birch, are the home of the Large Heath butterfly and the Rosy Marsh moths among others.

One of the fascinations of watching insects is that in a microhabitat or very small but well-defined area you can find dozens of specimens and several different species. For example, a cabbage plant can be the above-ground foodplant of six or more species of butterflies and moths and the below-ground food-source for as many moth larvae.

Plant specialists

The larvae of many species of fritillary butterflies feed only on plants of the violet family; dog-violets in wooded places are particular favourites. The rose family (hawthorn, apple, bramble, cinquefoil) also has its guild of butterflies and moths, including the Brown and Black Hairstreaks, Grizzled Skipper, Browntail moth and Lappet. Grasses, reeds and sedges provide food for most of the browns (e.g. Hermit, Meadow Brown, Small Heath, Marbled White), many of the skipper butterflies (e.g. Chequered and Large Skipper) and for numerous moth larvae including the wainscots, Antler and Gold Spot. Coniferous trees have a large group of specialists that includes the Pine Hawk-moth, Pine Processionary moth and the Spanish Moon-moth (not described in this book).

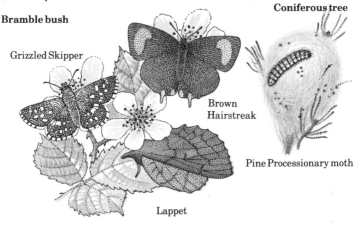

Coniferous tree

Bramble bush

Grizzled Skipper

Brown Hairstreak

Pine Processionary moth

Lappet

Some species are more fastidious and feed only on one genus of plants within a family: for example, on one of the oaks (Purple Hairstreak and Great Prominent moth), on species of *Primula* (Duke of Burgundy Fritillary) or on *Euphorbia* species (Spurge Hawk-moth). The White Admiral butterfly and the Broad-bordered Bee-Hawk moth larvae feed only on honeysuckles (*Lonicera*). Sometimes a single species of plant within a genus is chosen: for example, the Peacock, Red Admiral, Comma, Map, Small Tortoiseshell and the Gold Spangle and Snout moths nearly alway select nettle (*Urtica dioica*) as the foodplant. (The addiction of the South American Cactus moth to cactus plants made this species a dramatically useful friend of man in controlling prickly pear cactus in Australia.)

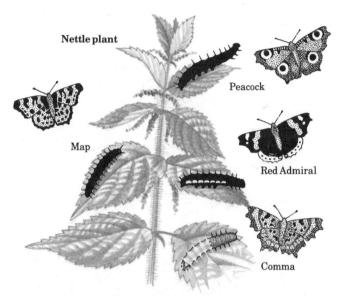

Nettle plant

Peacock

Map

Red Admiral

Comma

Primitive non-flowering plants like algae, fungi and lichens provide food for many hundreds of moth larvae, including most of the footmen moths.

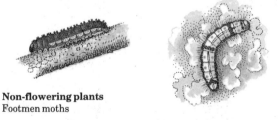

Non-flowering plants
Footmen moths

The flowers of some plants may form the temporary microhabitats for adult moths and butterflies. Buddleia flowers not only attract many day-flying butterflies like the Small Tortoiseshell, but at night are visited by Golden Plusias, Lesser Yellow Underwings and other moths. In the spring, the flowers of willows and sallows will attract the Swordgrass and Chestnut moths (not described) and others. Moths and butterflies therefore often act as pollinators, just like bees, as they fly from flower to flower.

Plant-parts specialists

Plant leaves provide food for most of the world's moth and butterfly larvae. Some minute leaf-mining larvae feed inside the tissues of the leaf, leaving signs of their activities on the surface of the leaf in the form of brown patches or bands. Other larvae (e.g. the Grizzled Skipper) draw together the edges of a leaf with silk and feed inside this shelter.

Leaf-mining larvae clue

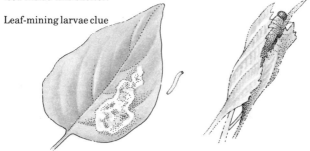

The Goat and Leopard moth larvae bore into trunks and branches of trees. The Currant Clearwing moth and Rosy Rustic moth larvae (not described) tunnel into stems of fairly soft-stemmed shrubs and other plants.

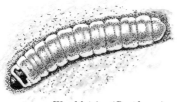
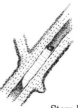

Wood-boring (Goat larva)   Stem-boring

Flowers, buds and fruits are attacked by larvae of the Holly Blue, Little Blue and of various moths including the Codling moth, Raspberry moth and the infamous pest-species the Corn Earworm (Scarce Bordered Straw).

Disliked by the farmer and gardener are underground larvae of the Turnip moth, Swift moth and others that attack the roots and tubers of plants.

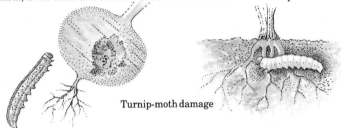

Turnip-moth damage

Unusual microhabitats
Sugar-secreting glands on the back of the larvae of the Large and Alcon Blue butterflies and some of their relatives are so attractive to ants that the ants take the larvae into their nest where they are tended throughout the winter, even though the butterfly larvae feed on the ant larvae.

The enterprising larvae of wax-moths feed on the waxy honeycombs inside bee-hives. Even more curious are the larvae of the small china-mark moths, which feed submerged on water plants. Opportunist house- and clothes-moth larvae feed either on woollen clothes or on particles of animal or vegetable matter trapped under skirting boards or on detritus in birds' nests, while in shops and warehouses the larvae of the Warehouse moth and others can become pests of stored foods.

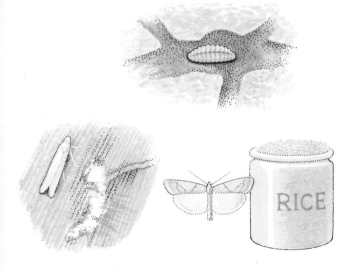

When and where
Some of the best places for butterflies and moths are mentioned under Habitats and Microhabitats (pages 14-19). However, do not forget to examine such places as disused railway cuttings, quarries, roadsides, the banks of rivers and lakes, and urban wasteland. Some of these restricted habitats can harbour a surprisingly large number of species. Moths, most of which are attracted to light at night, can be seen almost anywhere, especially if they are migratory species.

When to look for butterflies and moths is an easier question to answer. Most cold-blooded animals such as these move very little during cold weather, so there are few flying insects about during the winter. Exceptions are the Winter moth and one or two others. The best months for the butterfly watcher are from March to mid-October, with June, July and August as probably the most fruitful. However, the weather can often delay or bring forward the emergence of adults, so keep looking throughout the warmer months.

Larvae are likely to be active whenever there is available food. Many overwinter and start feeding again as soon as the plant leaves start to grow in the spring.

Footpath edged by old
hedgerows

Speckled Wood

Gatekeeper

Attracting

Many butterflies have to be looked for in their wild habitats, but flowery gardens, even in large towns, can attract several species of butterflies as well as moths (see also page 72I).

For at least some day-flying species you will need a collecting net so that you can examine and identify your visitors, and for day-flying moths you will need glass-bottomed pill-boxes (see also page 76).

At night, a bright lamp will attract many moths

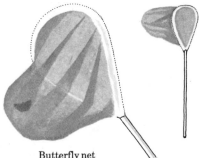

Butterfly net

Photography

Photographing adult and larval moths and butterflies can provide you with a permanent record of your discoveries, often with little disturbance to the subject of your photograph. You will need a single-lens reflex camera, with a special lens and perhaps extension tubes or bellows for close-up pictures. There are several excellent books on nature photography to which you should refer for more details.

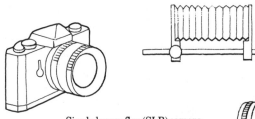

Single lens reflex (SLR) camera

Rearing

Rearing a species from the egg or larva to the adult stage is a particularly rewarding pastime (see page 74). Watching a species develop through the various stages provides a fascinating insight into an otherwise secret life. This is also one of the best ways of obtaining subjects for photography.

1   Flies by day: antennae clubbed or not ───────────── 2
    Flies at night; antennae not clubbed ───────────── 27
2   Antennae clubbed   3

    Antennae not clubbed   **26**

3   Wings at rest tent-like   Burnet moth p. 60

    Wings at rest vertical or spread   4

4   Wings white or yellow; may have dark markings ───────── 5
    Wings other than yellow or white ───────────── 13
5   Hind wings with large orange or red spots───────── 6
    Hind wings without such spots───────────── 7
6   Hind wings with tail   Swallowtail p. 30

    Hind wings without tail   Apollo p. 31

7   Underside of hind wings mottled ───────────── 8
    Underside of hind wings not mottled ───────────── 9

8 Forewings with large black central spot;
no orange areas

Bath White p. 34

Forewings with small black spot;
male forewings' tip orange

Orange-tip p. 33

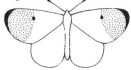

9 Underside of wings with black veins

(1) Black-veined White p. 31
(2) Green-veined White p. 33
(3) Marbled White p. 45

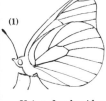 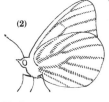

(1)   (2)   (3)

Veins of underside not black ───────────────── **10**

10 Wings yellow or orange, with red or brown markings ───────── **11**
Wings white, with black or grey markings ───────────── **12**

11 Angulate yellow wings

Brimstone p. 35

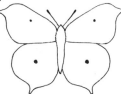

Rounded, brown-edged, orange wings

Clouded Yellow p. 34

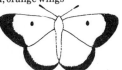

12 Flight weak and fluttery ———————————— Wood White p. 35
Flight fairly strong—————————————— Small White p. 32
Large White p. 32

13 Mostly brown with eye-spots; or small
blue, copper or brown species ————————— **21**
Not mostly brown, with or without eye-spots;
not small blue, copper or brown ————————— **14**

14 Colour-pattern intricate; mostly brown or orange ——— **15**
Colour-pattern not as above; variously coloured———— **16**

15 Underside of wings with eye-spots   (1) Wall p. 50
(2) Speckled Wood p. 50

Underside of wings without eye spots   (1) Fritillary pp. 42-44
(2) Map p. 41

16 All wings with white bands or edges   (1) Purple Emperor p. 37
(2) White Admiral p. 37
(3) Camberwell Beauty p. 38

Not as above ————————————————— **17**

17 Large species; mostly orange———————————— Monarch p. 36
Not as above ————————————————— **18**

18   Forewings with large white markings   (1) Red Admiral p. 39
(2) Painted Lady p. 40

(1)   **(2)**

Forewings without large white markings ———————— **19**
19   All wings with peacock-like markings   Peacock p. 39

Wings without such markings ———————————— **20**
20   Hind wings underside with white comma-like mark   Comma p. 41

Hind wings without comma-like mark   (1) Small Tortoiseshell p. 40
(2) Large Tortoiseshell p. 38

(1)   **(2)**

21   Upperside of wings without eye-spots ——————— **22**
Upperside and underside of wings
with eye-spots   Browns pp. 46–51

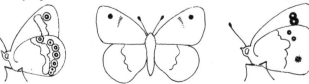

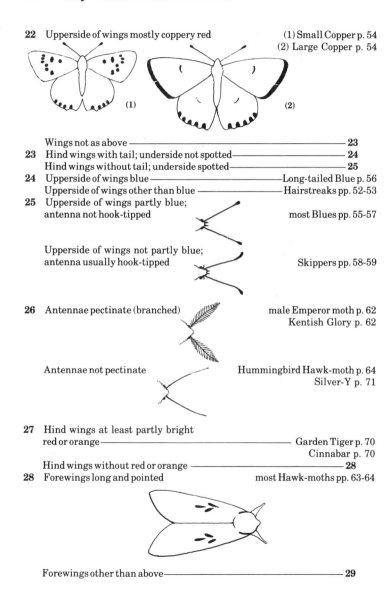

22 Upperside of wings mostly coppery red — (1) Small Copper p. 54
(2) Large Copper p. 54

Wings not as above ————————————————————————— **23**
23 Hind wings with tail; underside not spotted———————————— **24**
Hind wings without tail; underside spotted———————————— **25**
24 Upperside of wings blue ——————————————Long-tailed Blue p. 56
Upperside of wings other than blue ———————— Hairstreaks pp. 52-53
25 Upperside of wings partly blue;
antenna not hook-tipped — most Blues pp. 55-57

Upperside of wings not partly blue;
antenna usually hook-tipped — Skippers pp. 58-59

26 Antennae pectinate (branched) — male Emperor moth p. 62
Kentish Glory p. 62

Antennae not pectinate — Hummingbird Hawk-moth p. 64
Silver-Y p. 71

27 Hind wings at least partly bright
red or orange——————————————————————— Garden Tiger p. 70
Cinnabar p. 70
Hind wings without red or orange ————————————— **28**
28 Forewings long and pointed — most Hawk-moths pp. 63-64

Forewings other than above——————————————————— **29**

29 Wings mostly white and/or black —————————— **30**
　　Wings not as above ——————————————————— **33**
30 Forewings speckled or spotted————————————— **31**
　　Forewings striped or unmarked———————————— **32**
31 Wings with orange spots ⠀⠀⠀⠀⠀⠀⠀⠀⠀⠀⠀⠀⠀⠀⠀⠀ Magpie p. 66

Wings without orange spots ⠀⠀⠀⠀⠀⠀⠀⠀⠀⠀⠀ Peppered moth p. 67
⠀⠀⠀⠀⠀⠀⠀⠀⠀⠀⠀⠀⠀⠀⠀⠀⠀⠀⠀⠀⠀⠀⠀⠀⠀⠀⠀⠀ Leopard p. 60

32 Wings white; abdomen partly
　　yellowish brown ——————————————— Brown-tail p. 69
　　Wings striped, greyish white; abdomen
　　not as above——————————————————— Puss moth p. 68
33 Wings with large eye-spots or 'windows' ⠀⠀⠀ Kentish Glory p. 62
⠀⠀⠀⠀⠀⠀⠀⠀⠀⠀⠀⠀⠀⠀⠀⠀⠀⠀⠀⠀⠀⠀⠀⠀ female Emperor moth p. 62

　　Wings not as above ————————————————————— **34**
34 Body furry in appearance———————————————— **35**
　　Body not furry——————————————————————— **37**
35 Outer margins of wings scalloped ⠀⠀⠀⠀⠀⠀⠀⠀⠀⠀⠀ Lappet p. 61

Outer margins of wings not scalloped —————————————— **36**

36   Forewing apex with large brownish-yellow area   Buff-tip p. 68

Forewings not as above   (1) Pale Tussock p. 69
                                                                (2) Lobster p. 68
                                                                (3) Lackey p. 61

37   Wings at rest tent-like; fairly robust moths ———— Peach Blossom p. 65
                                                                Turnip moth p. 71
                                                                Grey Dagger p. 71
        Wings at rest not tent-like; less robust————————————————**38**
38   Males fly from October to December; female
        wings vestigial ————————————————————— Winter moth p. 66
        Flies in summer; females fully winged ————————————**39**
39   Forewings hooked;
        hind wings without tail   Oak Hook-tip p. 65

Forewings not hooked;
hind wings with tail   Swallow-tailed moth p. 67

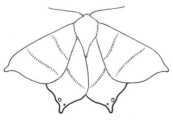

On the following Fact File pages, 57 species of butterfly and 26 species of moth are considered in detail. These are by no means all the butterflies and moths it is possible to see in the British Isles (where there are well over 60 species of butterfly and many more species of moth to be observed), but it does cover most of the common species and those easily recognized by a novice.

All butterflies and moths included in the book may be seen in Britain, and all occur on the continent, although sometimes there are regional distribution and colour differences. Most of the species described are residents in Britain, but a few are migrants and are here only for part of the year. This is noted in the text. Throughout the Fact File section species have been arranged according to natural (scientific) family groupings.

The information on each page is concise but clear and is designed to help you identify a butterfly or moth either by direct sighting of the caterpillar, pupa or adult insect or from its feeding signs. It is presented in the following standard format:

There is the *common* and *scientific* (Latin) *name* of the insect above a *description* of the species. The description includes the *range* of the species over the whole of northwest Europe. This is followed by details of *habitat*, explaining in general terms the types of countryside in which the insect is most likely to be seen. *Habits* includes where the adult and caterpillar feed, movement patterns, the annual life cycle from egg through caterpillar and pupa to adult and, where relevant, details of migration times and directions.

On each page usually one species is highlighted over and above another. the featured species bears a short descriptive text and three or four extra brief text descriptions of the adult, larva and pupa (and sometimes egg). Accompanying each text element is a picture of the subject – usually the adult shown in resting position and/or in flight, the caterpillar feeding or resting on its food source, the pupa in its resting place. All the illustrative elements are clustered on or around the insect's preferred food source or 'foodplant'.

A short selection like this obviously poses some problems. For example, visiting a wood or forest you may see many kinds of butterfly and moth which are not mentioned here. In just a few pages it is impossible to cover all the species you may see in such a situation. Also, depending on your location in Europe, the timing of events may be different. For example, in Scandinavia pupae will give rise to adult flying insects several weeks later than in, say, France simply because in spring the weather becomes warmer earlier the further south one is. But by making careful study of these common species you will at least get to know the behaviour patterns of the different major types of butterflies and moths and to learn something of several different but related species.

Emphasis here has been given to those clues, evidence and signs which are most easily seen. Clearly, if you take up the study of butterflies and moths (lepidoptera) in a more serious manner and become practised at examining specimens under a hand lens, then you will find there are more precise clues to look for and on which to base your identification. The more detailed descriptions of the species you will then require will be found in field guides and professional identification keys as found in such books as those listed under Further Reading on page 79.

Swallowtail *Papilio machaon*
Range Most of Europe. British resident in East
Anglia only.
Habitats Meadows, grassy mountain slopes and
moors, but restricted to Fenlands in Britain.
Habits Flies between April and August (May to June
in Britain). Graceful gliding flight. Eggs laid singly
on milk parsley in Britain, fennel and similar plants
in rest of Europe. Pupa overwinters on or near
foodplant.

Adult 60-90 mm. Pale
yellow wings, with
mostly black markings.
Red spot near base of
hind wing tail.

Pupa Usually green or
brown. Attached usually
head-upwards to
foodplant or nearby post.

Larva At first black and
white; later green with
black and orange rings.
When disturbed, pushes
out and up V-shaped
process behind head.

Larva Black with orange bands above; grey and white below. Many live together in a silken web, where they overwinter.

Black-veined white *Aporia crataegi*
Range Most warmer parts of Europe. Rare migrant to S. Britain.
Habitats Lucerne and clover fields, orchards, hedgerows and open woodland; often near water.
Habits Flies between May and July. Flight rather ungainly and slow. Lays batches of eggs, usually on blackthorn or hawthorn leaves but also on fruit trees where larvae can be pests.

Adult 58-68 mm. Male with conspicuous black veins on wings. Female wings more transparent and veins dark brown.

Pupa Green, grey and yellow-white, attached head-upwards to foodplant. Adults emerge after a few weeks.

Apollo *Parnassius apollo*
Range Mountains and hills of C. and S. Europe and in lowland areas of Scandinavia.
Habitats Open rocky or stony country, often near streams.
Habits Flies during July and August, feeding on thistle and other flowers. Flight usually slow and fluttery, but can glide gracefully. Eggs laid usually on stonecrops. Overwinters as small larva inside egg. Full-grown larva black, with grey-blue processes along back and orange spots along sides. Feeds only on sunny days. Pupa formed under a stone.

Adult 60-90 mm. White, slightly translucent wings with red, black and light grey markings.

Adult 56-68 mm. White wings with yellow underside and black and grey markings. Females more heavily marked.

Large white *Pieris brassicae*
Range Common in nearly all parts of Europe.
Habitats Pastures, meadows, gardens and farmland. Migrants can be seen everywhere.
Habits On the wing from April to September and easy to spot. Often attracted to lavender flowers. Eggs are laid in batches on cabbage, nasturtium and other cabbage-family plants. Often a pest in gardens. Usually has two or three broods each year.

Pupa Often pale green or yellow, with black markings. Attached to fence or tree trunk. Autumn pupae overwinter.

Larva Dull green, dotted with black and with yellow line along each side. Feeds in a group.

Adult 46-54 mm. White wings; dull yellow underside to hind wings.

Small white *Pieris rapae*
Range Most of Europe, and can be very common.
Habitats Meadows, gardens, farmlands; many other places during migration.
Habits Has two or three broods between March and October; commonest in midsummer. Eggs are laid singly on cabbage, hedge-mustard and other cabbage-family plants. Larva pale green, with three yellow lines; less conspicuous than Large white larvae. First brood pupae are green and attached to foodplant; later pupae variously coloured, attached to fences and walls. Autumn pupae overwinter.

Orange-tip *Anthocharis cardamines*
Range Most parts of Europe.
Habitats Woodland margins and clearings, flowery
hedgerows, occasionally in gardens.
Habits Can be seen feeding from flowers in sunshine
from April to June. Lays single eggs on cuckoo flower,
garlic mustard and other cabbage-family plants.
There is one brood each year.

Adult 34-48 mm. Males
have orange tips to
forewings; Females lack
orange but have large
black spot on forewings.

Pupa Distinctively
tapered; like long thorn.
Can be green, yellow or
brown. Overwinters.

Larva Green, spotted
with black and striped
with white. Will eat
flowers, seed pods and
leaves of plant.

Adult 38-50 mm. White
wings with black
markings, and with
green-lined veins on
underside.

Green-veined white *Pieris napi*
Range N. Scandinavia to Mediterranean.
Habitats Migratory and can be seen everywhere, but
most often in damp meadowland and along
hedgerows.
Habits Flies between April and early September,
usually in two broods. Often attracted to flowers.
Eggs are laid singly on hedge-mustard, charlock and
other cabbage-family plants. Larva pale green, with
dark green and yellow lines. Pupa green or brown;
often matches background foodplant, or nearby fence
or tree trunk. Autumn pupae overwinter.

Bath white *Pontia daplidice*
Range C. and S. Europe. Only as a migrant in
Britain and N. Europe.
Habitats Flowery meadows, pastures and hillsides,
often in dry areas.
Habits Found between April and August in two or
more broods. Often visits clover and other flowers. In
flight rather like female orange-tip. Eggs are laid
singly on hedge mustard and related plants. Full-
grown larvae are blue-grey, spotted with black and
striped with yellow. Pupae either green or brown,
with black markings; attached head-upwards to
foodplant. Spends winter either as larva or pupa.

Adult 40-50 mm. White
and black wings. Female
has extra black spot on
forewings.

Larva Green, marked
with rows of yellow, red
and black spots and
blotches. Autumn larvae
overwinter and pupate
in spring.

Pupa Usually green;
marked with brown,
yellow and black.
Attached head-upwards
to stem of plant.

Clouded yellow *Colias crocea*
Range Migrants breed in N. Europe but do not
overwinter. Resident throughout the year south of
the Alps.
Habitats Grassy places, heaths and in clover and
lucerne fields where flowers attract adults.
Habits Flies between February and October,
reaching N. Europe in late summer. Eggs are laid
singly on clovers, vetches and other pea-family
plants.

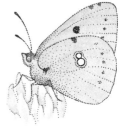

Adult 48-60 mm. Male
has orange wings,
female yellowish-white
ones; markings dark
brown, paler in female.

Brimstone *Gonepteryx rhamni*
Range Arctic to Mediterranean, but excluding Scotland.
Habitats Open woodland, heathland and old hedgerows. Sometimes seen in gardens.
Habits Appears as early as February or March after overwintering as adult. Strongly flying species; attracted to valerian, *Aubretia* and several wild flowers. Eggs laid singly, usually on buckthorn, less often on alder buckthorn. Only one brood each year.

Adult 50-62 mm. Male's wings lemon yellow above, female's much paler. Wing shape distinctive.

Pupa Green, with brown markings. Attached to foodplant or post nearby. Usually close to ground.

Larva Grey-green and bluish-green, with yellowish-white lines. Rests along mid-rib of leaf. Inconspicuous.

Wood white *Leptidea sinapis*
Range Most of Europe, including Arctic but not Scotland.
Habitats Woodland clearings and margins; also along sea cliffs in S.W. England.
Habits Flies from May to August. Flight weak and fluttery. Visits flowers and muddy puddles. Single eggs are laid on bird's foot trefoil, vetchlings and related plants. Larva green, with darker green line on the back and yellow line along each side. Pupa resembles shrivelled leaf and is attached head-upwards to foodplant. Autumn pupae overwinter.

Adult 35-46 mm. White wings with grey markings; more yellowish below.

Monarch *Danaus plexippus*
Range Known only as occasional migrant to Europe.
Habitats Flies in open flowery country; hibernates in colonies in trees.
Habits Celebrated migratory butterfly. Rare European specimens come from Canary Islands, where Monarch is resident, or from N. America. Single eggs are laid on milkweed plants, but on spurges in the Canaries.

Adult 75-100 mm. Orange wings with dark brown and white markings. Paler orange on underside.

Pupa Elegant, glossy green, with gold and black markings, suspended head-downwards on foodplant.

Larva Ringed with black, yellow and white. Two long black processes near head; two shorter processes at tail end.

Purple emperor *Apatura iris*

Range Much of Europe, as far north as Denmark and C. England.

Habitats Old oak woodlands, often near sallows.

Habits Flies in July and August; usually high up in oak trees, but may be attracted to mud or rotting animal matter on ground. Soaring, graceful flight. Eggs are laid singly on sallow or, less often, on poplar. Young larva overwinters attached to pad of silk, changing colour from green to brown.

Pupa Green and dark green. Attached to leaf, which in turn is fastened to twig with silk.

Larva Rather slug-like in shape. Green, with yellow stripes and red-tipped horns. Rests along leaf mid-rib.

Adult 64-80 mm. Male's wings brown with purple sheen above. Markings white and orange. Female's wings lack purple.

Adult 52-60 mm. Brown wings with white and darker brown markings.

White admiral *Ladoga camilla*

Range Most of Europe as far north as Sweden and C. England. Absent from Norway, the Netherlands and Ireland.

Habitats Deciduous woodlands, especially clearings and footpaths.

Habits June and July are the best months for this species. Will visit flowers and mud-puddles. Strong flight interspersed with gliding. Eggs are laid singly on honeysuckle or occasionally snowberry. Larva feeds at night and overwinters in rolled leaf attached to twig with silk. It is mostly green, with rows of spiny processes along back. Pupa green, brown and gold, with ear-like processes; looks like dead leaf.

Large tortoiseshell *Nymphalis polychloros*
Range Europe from Mediterranean to Scandinavia and C. England. Becoming rarer.
Habitats Woodland edges and clearings, old hedgerows and orchards.
Habits Most often seen in July and August, but also in autumn and again in early spring. Batches of eggs are laid on twigs of elms, sallows, fruit trees and others.

Adult 54-66 mm. Brownish-orange wings, with black and blue markings. The overwintering stage.

Pupa Formed about 2 m from ground. Mostly brown, with silver spots. Hangs head-downwards in crevice of bark.

Larva Many live in web. Black with dull orange lines. Has many black-tipped yellow spines.

Adult. 60-74 mm. Dark brown wings with dull blue spots and pale yellow margins.

Camberwell beauty *Nymphalis antiopa*
Range Much of Europe, especially central and south, also in Norway. Migrant to Britain and Ireland from Norway.
Habitats Usually found near trees, especially in marshy willow and birch areas.
Habits Powerful flight. Often visits tree sap and muddy puddles. Commonest in June and July, but flies as late as September and as early as March before and after hibernation. Eggs are laid in batches on twigs of willows, sallows, birch and other trees. Larvae black, with red markings and branched spines; feed in a communal web. Pupa is spiny, brown, suspended head-downwards from twig.

Adult 56-68 mm. Both sexes have reddish-orange wings with colourful eye-spots. Underside of wings a contrasting dull brown.

Larva Lives in group in a web. Feeds mostly on young shoots. Black, with white dots and branched black spines.

Peacock *Inachis io*
Range Most of Europe except far north of Scandinavia.
Habitats Common in gardens and other places with flowers, including orchards, meadows, hedgerows and wasteland.
Habits Overwinters as an adult and can be seen in late autumn and early spring. Commonest from July to September, feeding from thistle, ice-plant and other flowers. Frequently opens and closes wings. Eggs are laid in batches, usually on nettle. Has a single brood each year.

Pupa Hangs head-downwards from branch or fence. Variously coloured; with gold sheen. Two-horned head.

Adult 56-88 mm. Nearly black wings with orange-red and white markings.

Red admiral *Vanessa atalanta*
Range Resident in most of Europe, but mainly a migrant in Britain and N. Scandinavia.
Habitats Gardens, woodland clearings, parks and orchards.
Habits Commonest in midsummer when migrants from S. Europe move northwards, but overwinters as an adult and therefore also appears in autumn and spring. Visits flowers, rotting fruit and sap. Eggs are laid singly, usually on nettle. Larva almost black, with white spots, yellow side-line and branched red-brown spines. Pupa greyish-brown, with golden spots; attached head-upwards. One brood each year.

Small tortoiseshell *Aglais urticae*
Range All of Europe, including the far north and up to an altitude of 3500 m on mountains.
Habitats Most open countryside where there are flowers. Common in gardens and parks.
Habits Overwinters as adult and in Britain flies as early as March. May have two broods during the summer. Visits flowers and often basks in sun. Large batches of eggs are laid on young shoots of nettle. Usually chooses nettle beds in fairly open positions.

Adult 44-52 mm.
Reddish-orange wings, with dark brown, yellow and blue markings. Underside brown and dull yellow.

Larva Feeds in group inside a web. Yellow and black, with green and black branched spines.

Pupa Pinkish-grey, with gold markings. Hangs head-downwards from fencing or post.

Painted lady *Cynthia cardui*
Range Regular migrant to most of N. Europe but overwinters only in S. Europe.
Habitats Any open country where there are flowers.
Habits Arrives in N. Europe in May and June, and produces second brood in July and August. Some migrate southwards in autumn. Will visit garden flowers and many wild flowers. Single eggs are laid usually on thistle or burdock. Larva makes small web under leaf. It is black or dark grey, with white dots, yellow along sides and has many black, or yellow and black, branched spines. Pupa is grey, often with gold or copper markings and is suspended head-downwards from a leaf.

Adult 54-64 mm.
Orange wings, with dark brown and white markings.

Adult 44-54 mm. Wing shape distinctive. Wings orange and dark brown above. Dull brown beneath, with white comma.

Comma *Polygonia c-album*
Range Much of Europe, but not N. Britain or Scandinavia.
Habitats Edges of woods, old hedgerows, gardens, meadows and wastelands.
Habits Spends winter as adult, so can be on wing in early summer and autumn. Commonest in July and August. Two broods each year. Visits flowers and also attracted to rotting fruit. Single eggs are laid, usually on nettle but also on bramble, hops, elm and other plants.

Larva Feeds alone under a light web. Black, with yellow or red on sides, white patch on back and branched yellow spines.

Pupa Varies in colour; often pink, black and green, with silvery spots. Hangs head-downwards from foodplant.

Map *Araschnia levana*
Range C. and parts of N. Europe, but not Britain, Norway or Sweden.
Habitats Forest clearings and pathways; especially on damp soils.
Habits First brood flies between April and June, second between mid-July and September. Often rests on ground or foliage in sunshine. Chains of eggs, laid on nettle, look like nettle flowers or fruits. Larvae feed in a group on nettle leaves and shoots; they are black or yellowish-brown, with yellow stripes and spots and with many-branched black or yellow spines. Pupa brown or green, sometimes with silvery spots. Suspended head-downwards from foodplant.

Adult 32-44 mm. First brood have mostly orange wings; second mostly black. Underside reticulate and map-like.

Silver-washed fritillary *Argynnis paphia*
Range Most of Europe, but not Scotland or N.
Scandinavia.
Habitats Woodland edges and clearings, or old
hedgerows with trees.
Habits Most often seen in July and August.
Attracted to flowers of bramble, thistles, dandelion
and others. Powerful flight. Eggs are laid singly on
south-facing trunks of oak or other trees. Larva
hatches but remains in bark crevice throughout
winter, descending in spring to feed on violets.

Pupa Yellowish-brown,
with dark brown and
gold markings.
Suspended head-
downwards on plant.

Larva Dark brown lined
with yellow, and with
several black-tipped
brown spines.

Adult 56-74 mm. Male's
wings orange and black;
female's more strongly
marked. Undersides
with silvery streaks.

Adult 50-64 mm.
Orange wings, with
black markings above;
silver spots beneath.

High brown fritillary *Fabriciana adippe*
Range Much of Europe, but not in Scotland or N.
Scandinavia.
Habitats Generally a woodland species.
Habits Flies from June to August. Visits flowers.
Single eggs laid on violets. Young larva stays in shell
during winter. Full grown larva variable in colour;
with branched spines. Pupa brown, with green and
gold markings.

Small pearl-bordered fritillary *Clossiana selene*
Range Most of Europe, except for Arctic and S. Spain
and Italy.
Habitats Damp woodland meadows (Britain), moors
and grassy hillsides near forests.
Habits Two broods in S. Europe, usually one in N.,
flying during June and July. Usually flies close to
ground. Single eggs are laid on violets. Autumn
larvae overwinter, partly grown, in curled leaf sealed
with silk.

Adult 34-44 mm. Wings
orange and dark brown
above, intricately
patterned beneath with
yellow or silvery spots.

Larva Brown, with
white dots and many
hairy yellow-brown
processes along back and
sides.

Pupa Blue-brown, with
black and silver spots.
Hangs head-downwards
from leaf or stem of
foodplant.

Adult 32-44 mm. Wings
orange and brown above;
orange, black and yellow
below.

Glanville fritillary *Melitaea cinxia*
Range Channel Is. and Isle of Wight in Britain but
widely distributed elsewhere except for extreme S.
and N. of Europe.
Habitats Meadows, pastures and south-facing
grassy hillsides.
Habits On the wing in May and June in N. Europe.
Attracted to flowers of dandelion family and others.
Batches of eggs are laid on plantains, hawkweeds and
other plants. Larvae feed in a group and overwinter
in silken web. Full grown larva black, spotted with
white and with many brownish-green, black-haired
processes. Pupa variable in colour; hangs head-
downwards from foodplant or nearby plants or rocks.

Marsh fritillary *Eurodryas aurinia*
Range Rare in Britain, less so elsewhere in Europe.
Absent from N. Scandinavia.
Habitats Marshes, damp moors, meadows and
hillsides up to 3000 m.
Habits Can be seen in May and June, rarely later.
Forms colonies and locally can be quite common.
Eggs are laid in batches on devil's-bit scabious,
speedwells and plantains. Larvae live in a group
under a web and overwinter partly grown.

Pupa Hangs head-
downwards from
foodplant or on nearby
fence. Black and pale
yellow with orange
knobs on sides.

Adult 34-46 mm. Wing
colour varies. Usually
orange, black and yellow
above; paler beneath.

Larva Black, with white
dots and several rows of
black processes along
back and sides.

Heath fritillary *Mellicta athalia*
Range Common in much of Europe; in Britain
restricted to a few colonies in S. England.
Habitats Newly cut clearings in woodland or on
moors, heaths and in meadows.
Habits Flies in June and July, usually keeping close
to ground. Batches of eggs are laid, usually on cow-
wheats, plantains or speedwells. Larvae feed and
overwinter in communal web until full grown. They
are black, spotted with white and with several black-
haired white processes along body. Pupa black and
white, with orange processes on back; hangs upside-
down from foodplant or on nearby fence.

Adult 36-42 mm. Wings
orange and dark brown
above, much paler
below.

Grayling *Hipparchia semele*
Range Throughout Europe except for N. Scandinavia and S. Italy.
Habitats Heaths, moors, sand dunes, sea cliffs and dry grassland.
Habits Flies from July to early September, visiting thyme and other flowers, but often rests on ground with wings inclined towards sun so that little shadow is cast. Single eggs are laid on tufted hair-grasses and other grasses. Young larva overwinters at base of foodplant, feeding again in early spring.

Larva Yellow-brown, with darker brown lines along body. Well hidden among grasses.

Adult 48-60 mm. Brown and pale orange wings, with black and white eye-spots above. Paler with more white below.

Pupa Red-brown in colour. Lies just below soil surface in cocoon of silk and soil.

Adult 46-56 mm. Wings white and dark brown above, paler below.

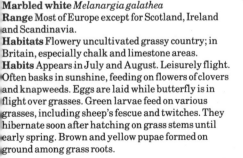

Marbled white *Melanargia galathea*
Range Most of Europe except for Scotland, Ireland and Scandinavia.
Habitats Flowery uncultivated grassy country; in Britain, especially chalk and limestone areas.
Habits Appears in July and August. Leisurely flight. Often basks in sunshine, feeding on flowers of clovers and knapweeds. Eggs are laid while butterfly is in flight over grasses. Green larvae feed on various grasses, including sheep's fescue and twitches. They hibernate soon after hatching on grass stems until early spring. Brown and yellow pupae formed on ground among grass roots.

Adult 48-54 mm. Wings orange and brown above. Underside paler, with irregular white line across hind wings.

Arran brown *Erebia ligea*
Range Probably never present on Isle of Arran. Resident in parts of C. Europe and in Scandinavia.
Habitats Grassy hillsides and meadows near woodlands above 300 m.
Habits Flies between late June and August. Flight rather jerky in character. Single eggs are laid on meadow grasses, millets and other grasses. Larvae enter hibernation either just before hatching or soon after; some feed for two summers before changing into pupa.

Larva Yellow-grey, with dark line on back and pale line along each side.

Pupa Light brown, with black markings. Formed on ground among grass roots.

Adult 40-52 mm. Wings dark brown and yellowish-white above; larger pale areas below.

Hermit *Chazara briseis*
Range Found in N.E. France but otherwise a S. and C. European species.
Habitats Rough, stony grassland, especially on chalk and limestone hills.
Habits Can be seen between June and September, occasionally visiting flowers. Eggs are laid on blue moor grass, fescues and other grasses. Young larvae overwinter on foodplant; full grown larvae are yellowish-grey, with dark grey lines along back and four pale grey lines on sides. Pupa brown, with dark brown lines along back; formed near surface of soil at base of grasses.

Ringlet *Aphantopus hyperantus*
Range Widely distributed in most of Europe.
Habitats Woodland clearings and pathways, old
hedgerows and, less often, damp meadowland and
marshes.
Habits Appears in July in the north, between June
and August elsewhere. Somewhat undulating flight.
Often visits flowers. Eggs scattered over foodplants:
cocksfoot, meadow grasses, twitches, other grasses
and sedges. Larva overwinters and usually feeds
throughout winter. Single brood each year.

Pupa Yellow-brown,
with reddish-brown
markings. Seen on the
ground in cocoon of silk
and grass roots.

Adult 40-50 mm. Wings
dark brown above, paler
below. Eye-spots black;
some with white centres.
Female paler.

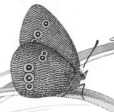

Larva Yellow-brown,
with dark brown line on
back and pinkish-white
line on each side.

Scotch argus *Erebia aethiops*
Range W. & S. Scotland, N.W. England, coastal
Belgium and mountains of C. Europe.
Habitats Usually on grassy slopes or moors close to
coniferous woodlands.
Habits Flies in July and August in sunshine but also
in dull weather if warm enough. Single eggs are laid
on various grasses. Young larvae overwinter among
grass roots, feeding again in spring. Full grown larva
usually yellow-brown, striped with dull yellow and
dark brown. Pupa brownish-yellow with black
markings; hidden among grass roots in frail cocoon of
silk, soil and roots.

Adult 40-52 mm. Wings
mostly orange and
brown. Eye-spots black
and white.

Meadow brown *Maniola jurtina*
Range Common in most of Europe – to an altitude of about 2000 m.
Habitats Hedgerows, meadows, gardens, marshes, wherever there are flowers and grass.
Habits Flies from June to October. Often on the wing in dull weather, unlike most butterflies, and is attracted to flowers. Eggs are laid singly on meadow grasses and other grasses. Larva less active in winter but continues to feed. Has single brood each year.

Adult 44-50 mm. Male's wings red-brown, with black and white eye-spots; paler beneath. Female's forewings more orange.

Pupa Green and yellow, marked with black and brown. Hangs head-downwards from grass stem.

Larva Yellow-green spotted with black; dark green line along back and yellow-white line on each side.

Adult 36-42 mm. Orange and reddish-brown wings; eye-spots black and white.

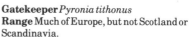

Gatekeeper *Pyronia tithonus*
Range Much of Europe, but not Scotland or Scandinavia.
Habitats Hedgerows, wasteland, edges of woods, meadows, heaths and moors.
Habits Most often seen in July and August. Often feeds on bramble and other flowers. Single eggs are laid on cocksfoot, meadow grasses and others. Larva brownish-green or yellow, with dark line on back and white line on each side. Usually feeds only at night, resting at base of grass by day. Overwinters from October onwards. Pupa green or brown, marked with black and brown; hangs head-downwards from grass. There is a single brood each year.

Pupa Green, streaked with brown and dark green. Hangs head-downwards from foodplant.

Larva Green with darker green lines, dotted with white above and black below.

Adult 35-40 mm. Wings mostly reddish-brown, with black and white eye-spots.

Small heath *Coenonympha pamphilus*
Range Nearly all of Europe, but absent from Orkney and Shetland islands.
Habitats Grassy places everywhere, especially meadows, heaths and moors.
Habits Usually has two broods each year between May and October, except in north where there is a single shorter flight period. Seldom flies far if disturbed. Eggs are laid singly near base of fescues, meadow grasses and others. Some larvae overwinter and continue to feed during warm weather; others pupate in autumn.

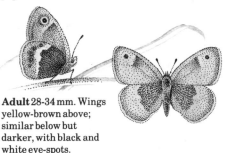

Adult 28-34 mm. Wings yellow-brown above; similar below but darker, with black and white eye-spots.

Large heath *Coenonympha tullia*
Range C. and N. Europe, including Scotland, C. and N. Wales and England.
Habitats Peat bogs, wet moorland and meadows.
Habits Adults can be seen between June and August. Usually keeps close to ground among vegetation. Seldom visits flowers. Eggs are laid singly on cotton grasses, sedges and related plants. Larva overwinters, when partly grown, at base of foodplant. Full grown larva is green, with white and pink processes, and striped with dark green and white. Pupa suspended head-downwards from foodplant; it is bright green, marked with white and dark green.

Speckled wood *Pararge aegeria*
Range Found in most of Europe except for
Scandinavia.
Habitats Clearings and edges of woodlands and
along shady hedgerows and lanes.
Habits Often has two or three broods each year; on
the wing from April to September. Well camouflaged
among foliage on sunny days but also flies in dull
weather. Single eggs are laid on melic, cocksfoot,
couch and other grasses. Overwinters either as larva
or pupa.

Pupa Brown or green,
dotted with white and
marked with brown and
black. Hangs head-
downwards from grass.

Larva Green, dotted
with white; darker green
band on back and yellow
lines on sides.

Adult 34-46 mm. Wings
dark brown and yellow
above, with black and
white eye-spots. Paler
beneath.

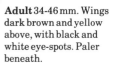

Adult 36-40 mm.
Mainly brown and
orange above, paler
beneath.

Wall *Lasiommata megera*
Range Much of Europe, but excluding N. Scotland
and N. Scandinavia.
Habitats Dry sunny gardens, waste ground,
hedgerows, heaths, moors and roadsides.
Habits May have up to three broods each year and
flies between April and September. Often rests on
ground or a wall, basking in sunshine, but is also
attracted to garden and wild flowers. Eggs are laid
singly on cocksfoot, meadow grasses and others.
Bluish-green, white-striped larvae usually feed only
at night. Autumn larvae either hibernate or continue
to feed during winter. Pupae vary in colour but are
usually speckled with white and have two rows of
small white processes; suspended head-downwards
from grass stems.

Large wall brown *Lasiommata maera*
Range Found from Mediterranean to Arctic but absent from Britain, Denmark and much of N. Germany.
Habitats Stony grassy countryside, often near woods.
Habits Flies from June to August, usually having one brood each year. Often rests on rocks, basking in sunshine. Single eggs are laid on fescues and on several other grasses. Autumn larvae overwinter at base of foodplant.

Larva Pale green, with pale-edged dark green lines on back and sides.

Pupa Usually green, with two lines of yellow processes. Hangs head-downwards from foodplant.

Adult 44-54 mm. Male's wings brown and orange above; female's with large pale areas. Eye-spots black and white. Underside paler.

Adult 48-54 mm. Wings brown above with yellow-edged black eye-spots. Similar below with yellow lines and white-centred eye-spots.

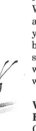

Woodland brown *Lopinga achine*
Range. France, Belgium, S.E. Sweden and C. Germany.
Habitats Margins of woods and in clearings especially where there is hazel; usually in deciduous woods, less often in mixed deciduous and coniferous woodland.
Habits On the wing between June and August; often rests on tree leaves or on grass. Egg-laying behaviour not known. Larval foodplants include false brome, rye, meadow and melic grasses. Larva overwinters at base of grass. Pupa green, lined with white, and with four white processes.

Adult 24-29 mm. Male's wings with purple sheen to forewings. Female's wings faintly purple. Underside pale brown, with orange spots.

Purple hairstreak *Quercusia quercus*
Range Most of Europe except for Scotland and N. Scandinavia.
Habitats Oak woodland and oak scrub; up to 2000 m.
Habits Adults appear between June and early September. Usually restricted to upper branches of trees, but attracted to honeydew, flowering plants and tree sap closer to ground. Eggs are laid singly on or near oak buds, rarely other trees; overwintering until April. Larva spins light web over buds and shoots. Pupa is formed inside frail silk cocoon on bark or leaf.

Larva Brown, with pale triangular marks along back and dark dashes along sides.

Pupa Shiny brownish-red, spotted with dark brown.

Adult 28-34 mm. Wings orange and brown above; orange, white and brown below.

Duke of Burgundy fritillary *Hamearis lucina*
Range S., C. and parts of N. Europe, but excluding Scotland, Norway, Holland, and N.W. Germany.
Habitats Pathways and clearings in forests, often where hazel is present; in Britain, prefers limestone areas.
Habits Appears in May and June. Flight rapid, rather like that of skippers. Usually rests on leaves. Two or three eggs are laid together on cowslip or primrose leaves. Hairy larva is tapered at both ends; brown with black spots along back and brown dashes along sides; feeds underneath leaves. Pupa brown, spotted with black; attached head-upwards to foodplant. Overwinters as a pupa.

White-letter hairstreak *Strymonidia w-album*
Range Most of Europe, but excluding N.
Scandinavia and whole of Scotland. Rare in the
Netherlands.
Habitats Woodland and tree-lined roads, especially
where there are wych-elms.
Habits Appears in July and August, usually flying
among branches of trees but may be attracted to
bramble flowers. Eggs – the overwintering stage –
are laid in fork of wych-elm, ash or lime twig.

Larva Usually yellow-
green, with furrowed
back and pale yellow
lines. Each segment
bears a pair of humps.

Pupa Brownish-yellow,
with brown markings
and numerous white
bristles. Pupates on leaf
or twig.

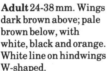

Adult 24-38 mm. Wings
dark brown above; pale
brown below, with
white, black and orange.
White line on hindwings
W-shaped.

Adult 25-30 mm. Wings
brown above, green on
underside.

Green hairstreak *Callophrys rubi*
Range Throughout Europe, including the Arctic.
Habitats Woodland edges and clearings, heaths and
moors with birch, old hedgerows; less often on moors
and bogs.
Habits On the wing from April to July. Often settles
on leaves, where green underside of wings gives
perfect camouflage. Flies strongly. Eggs are laid
singly on buds or shoots of gorse, broom, heather,
bilberry and other plants. Slug-like, hairy, furrowed,
mostly green larva feeds inside flower buds and
fruits. Pupa, which can produce squeaking sounds, is
brown marked with black and covered with short
hairs; formed on ground at base of foodplant, where it
overwinters.

Small copper *Lycaena phlaeas*
Range Widespread in most of Europe.
Habitats Wasteland, dry pastures and meadows, heaths, moors, gardens and parks.
Habits Up to four broods each year in N. Europe; on the wing from April to October. Flies rapidly from flower to flower. Males chase away other butterflies from their territory. Single eggs are laid usually on sorrels and docks. Autumn larvae hibernate on foodplant.

Larva Green with hairy white processes. May have pink markings. Head withdrawn unless feeding.

Adult 25-30 mm. Wings glossy reddish-orange and dark brown above. Much paler below, without orange on hindwings.

Pupa Yellow-brown, marked with brown and black. Fastened to stem or leaf of foodplant.

Adult 34-40 mm. Wings reddish-orange and brown above, paler and spotted below.

Large copper *Lycaena dispar*
Range France, the Netherlands, Germany and C. Europe. British fenland populations were introduced from the Netherlands.
Habitats Marshes and fens with sedges and reeds. Becoming more rare in Europe as land is drained for farming.
Habits In England and the Netherlands, appears during June and July. Elsewhere usually has two broods and is on the wing from May to September. Eggs are laid singly or in small batches on great waterdock or other dock plants. Larva hairy, green, with dark lines and with pairs of white-tipped knobs on back. Overwinters in folded leaf and can be submerged without ill effects. Honey glands on back attract ants. Pupa yellow-brown, spotted with white and black.

Larva Feeds at night on shoots, flowers and fruits. Green or greenish-yellow.

Holly blue *Celastrina argiolus*
Range Widely distributed in Europe but absent from Scotland and N.W. Scandinavia.
Habitats Woodland clearings, scrubland, heaths, gardens, old hedgerows and parks.
Habits Flies from March to June, often with second-brood flight in July and September. Flies strongly. Rests on leaves and attracted to sap and muddy puddles, seldom flowers. Eggs are laid singly on flower buds of holly, ivy, buckthorn, gorse or other shrubs.

Adult 22-32 mm. Male's wings mostly light blue above; female's with dark brown margins. Pale blue spotted with black below.

Pupa Brown, with darker marks. Attached to foodplant. Autumn pupae overwinter.

Adult 18-26 mm. Female's wings brown, male's blue and brown above. Pale blue, spotted with black below.

Little blue *Cupido minimus*
Range Much of Europe but excluding N. Scandinavia.
Habitats Dry meadows, pastures and roadsides, especially in chalk or limestone areas; less often on sand dunes.
Habits Usually appears in June, but may have second-brood flight in August. Often forms small colonies. Attracted to flowers. Single eggs are laid on flower buds of kidney vetch or related plants. Slug-shaped larva only 5 mm long; green or yellow, with black head and pink lines: feeds on flowers and seeds and overwinters in web among dead flower heads. Honey gland on abdomen attracts ants. Pupa brown, spotted with dark brown; attached to grass stem or foodplant.

Adult 35-40 mm. Wings of both sexes blue and black above; mostly pale brown beneath, spotted with black.

Large blue *Maculinea arion*
Range C. and S. Europe. Absent from Norway and N. Sweden. Recently became extinct in Britain.
Habitats Dry grassland and moors, where foodplant, thyme, is present.
Habits Flies in June and July and perhaps August. Eggs are laid singly on flower buds. Young larvae are collected by ants, which are attracted to the larval honey glands, and are fed by the ants in their nest. Larvae pupate in the nest and emerge as adult butterflies in the following spring.

Pupa Brownish-white. Formed in spring inside ants' nest.

Larva While feeding on thyme, brownish-pink; later inside ants' nest, becomes nearly white.

Adult 24-36 mm. Male's wings blue above, female's mostly brown. Brown and white below.

Long-tailed blue *Lampides boeticus*
Range Resident in S. Europe; migrant to N. Europe, including England, where another brood may be produced.
Habitats Open uncultivated areas with fairly lush vegetation and arable farmland.
Habits Has no hibernating stage and therefore needs larval foodplants throughout the year. Flies in S. Europe from June to October, usually visiting N. Europe later in summer. Eggs are laid singly on flower buds of cultivated peas and beans and on wild pea-family plants. Larva green, with honey gland on back that attracts ants. Pupa pale yellow and brown; in frail cocoon in curled leaf of foodplant.

Common blue *Polyommatus icarus*
Range Throughout Europe.
Habitats Flowery meadows, heaths, moors and sand dunes; wherever larval foodplants are present.
Habits Flies between May and October. Can be very common at times. Usually has two broods each year, sometimes three. Single eggs are laid on bird's foot trefoil, horseshoe vetches, clovers and other pea-family plants. Autumn larvae overwinter on foodplant in a silk shelter.

Adult 25-33 mm. Male's wings blue above, female's brown and orange. Pale brown below, with white, black and orange spots.

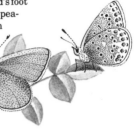

Larva Green, with dark line on back and yellow line on each side. Head black. Feeds on leaves and flowers.

Pupa Green, marked with brown. Formed in cocoon on ground at base of foodplant.

Chalk-hill blue *Lysandra coridon*
Range Locally common in C. and S. Europe except for Spain and S. Italy; absent from Scotland, Scandinavia and Portugal.
Habitats Chalk and limestone grassland, especially hilly areas.
Habits Appears between mid-July and mid-September. Attracted to flowers and animal droppings. Single eggs are laid on stems of horseshoe vetch and other pea-family plants. Young larva remains in egg throughout winter; later feeds at night on leaves and flowers. Full grown larva green, lined with yellow; honey gland on back attracts ants, which may carry larva to new foodplant. Pupa dull yellow marked with brown, formed on ground among roots of foodplant.

Adult 30-36 mm. Male's wings mostly blue above, female's brown. Pale brown with white-edged black spots below.

Grizzled skipper *Pyrgus malvae*
Range Most of Europe, but not Scotland, N. England or arctic Scandinavia.
Habitats Grassy hillsides (especially on chalk downs), meadows, woodland clearings and bogs.
Habits May be on the wing from April to September in two broods or have only single flight in May and June. Rests on ground, grass and flowers. Eggs laid singly on silverweed, wild strawberry and other rose-family plants. Autumn pupae overwinter in cocoon at or near base of foodplant.

Adult 20-28 mm. Wings dark brown and yellowish-white above, reddish-brown and yellowish-white below.

Larva Protected inside rolled leaf. Mostly green marked with brown lines, and with a black head.

Pupa Brown and green. Hidden inside rolled leaf. Held in place with silk.

Adult 26-29 mm. Wings orange and brown above; yellow and orange below.

Chequered skipper *Carterocephalus palaemon*
Range Most of Europe from Alps to Arctic Circle, but not at high altitudes. Probably became extinct in England in 1975.
Habitats Damp woodland meadows. Less often found on more open damp grassland.
Habits Appears between mid-May and early July. Flies swiftly but often basking in sunshine on ground and visits flowers. Single eggs are laid on brome, false brome and other grasses. Greenish-yellow larva makes tubular shelter of grass and silk; overwinters and then pupates in spring without feeding again. Pupa pale yellow and brown.

Large skipper *Ochlodes venatus*
Range Most of Europe, but absent from N. Scotland and N. Scandinavia.
Habitats Meadows, grassy hillsides and woodland clearings.
Habits Can be seen from late May to August. Fast flight. Will rest on ground and visit flowers. Males chase away other butterflies from their territory. Eggs are laid singly on various grasses and occasionally on rushes. Larva overwinters in tubular shelter of grass and silk, feeding again in spring. Pupa protected inside cocoon of grass blades bound with silk. Has one brood each year.

Pupa Dark grey and green, with short yellow hairs. Proboscis case not fused to body.

Adult 27-35 mm. Wings brownish-orange and brown above; similar in pattern beneath, but paler.

Larva Green and blue-green, with dark line on back and pale lines on sides. Head yellow and brown.

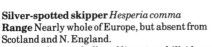

Silver-spotted skipper *Hesperia comma*
Range Nearly whole of Europe, but absent from Scotland and N. England.
Habitats Grassy chalk and limestone hillsides and dry meadows.
Habits Appears in July and August; flies rapidly, usually close to ground. Rests on ground or leaves and is attracted to thistle and other flowers. Single eggs are laid on fescues and other grasses, where they remain throughout the winter. Green and black larva makes tubular shelter of silk and grass. Pupa green and yellow, with black markings on head and thorax; found inside cocoon of silk and grass at base of foodplant.

Adult 28-32 mm. Wings mostly orange and brown; silvery spots beneath.

Six-spot burnet *Zygaena filipendulae*
Range Most of Europe, including Britain and
Scandinavia.
Habitats Grassy chalk and limestone hills,
meadows, sand dunes and marshes.
habits Flies from late May to July or August. Slow
bee-like flight, in sunshine. Eggs are laid in batches
on bird's foot trefoil, vetches and other pea-family
plants. Like other burnets is known to contain
cyanide-like substances in its tissues and is
poisonous to most birds and mammals.

Larva Yellowish-green,
with black and yellow
markings. Overwinters
on foodplant and feeds
again in spring.

Adult 28-34 mm. Wings
blue-black with crimson
spots, blue-black body.
Antennae slightly
swollen and hooked at
the tip.

Pupa Brown, protected
by delicate, tapered silk
cocoon placed near top of
grass stem.

Adult 50-64 mm. Wings
and body blue-black and
white. Female with
pointed ovipositor.

Leopard moth *Zeuzera pyrina*
Range Most of Europe, including the British Isles, in
particular S. England.
Habitats Wherever there are large trees: woods,
orchards, parks, gardens and tree-lined roads.
Habits Appears in June, July and August. Flies at
night but may be seen resting on tree-trunks during
the day. Eggs are laid in small crevices in bark of
fruit trees, plane, sycamore and others. Brownish
white larva lives under bark then burrows into trunk
and branches. Reddish droppings under a tree may be
a clue to the presence of larva. Larval stage usually
lasts for two years. Reddish-brown pupa formed close
to bark in cocoon of silk and chewed wood.

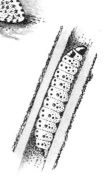

Lackey *Malacosoma neustria*
Range Throughout Europe except for Scotland and
N. Scandinavia.
Habitats Heaths with a few trees, open woodland,
orchards, old gardens and hedgerows.
Habits Appears between June and September, flying
at night. Eggs, which overwinter, are laid on twigs of
hawthorn, blackthorn, fruit trees and various other
trees. Larvae live in groups inside conspicuous white
web spun over leaves. Pupa brown, formed inside
cocoon attached to foodplant. Inner wall of cocoon
powdered with yellow.

Adult 25-38 mm.
Yellowish- or reddish-
brown body and wings,
with darker lines or
broader dark band on
wings.

Eggs Always in a band
round twig. Up to 200
eggs in one batch.

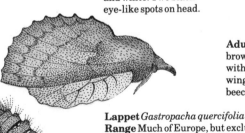

Larva Greyish-blue,
striped with red, black
and white. Two black
eye-like spots on head.

Adult 40-78 mm. Red-
brown body and wings,
with dark lines on
wings. Resembles dead
beech leaf.

Lappet *Gastropacha quercifolia*
Range Much of Europe, but excluding Scotland.
Habitats Woodlands, orchards and old hedgerows.
Habits Flies at night. On the wing in June and July
in north, and from May to August in two broods in
south. Eggs are laid in small batches under leaves of
hawthorn, blackthorn, sallow and fruit trees. Larva
bluish-grey or brown, with hairy, fleshy processes
(lappets) along sides and with blue spots. Can be pest
in S. European orchards. Overwinters when small,
low down on foodplant. Dark brown pupa formed on
foodplant inside cocoon of silk and larval hairs.

Emperor *Eudia pavonia*
Range Europe from Arctic to Mediterranean.
Habitats Moors and heaths, but also at margins of woodlands.
Habits Flies between April and June. Males fly in afternoon sunshine looking for females, but females do not take to wing until dusk. Eggs are laid in band round twig or stem of heather, blackthorn, bramble, bilberry and other plants. Pupa may overwinter for two winters.

Adult 52-70 mm. Body and wings mainly grey and brown, with white and black bands and spots. Female lacks yellow tinge to hind wings.

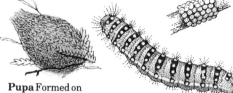

Pupa Formed on foodplant inside silk cocoon, which has one-way exit hole for emerging moth.

Larva Green, with black rings and yellow or pink process on each segment.

Kentish glory *Endromis versicolora*
Range Throughout Europe, but in Britain now restricted to Scotland.
Habitats Heaths and moors with birch, and in open woodland.
Habits On the wing from late March to end of May. Males fly by day, females only at night. Well-camouflaged when at rest on birch bark. Eggs are laid in short rows on twigs of birch or less often on hazel, lime and other trees. Larvae feed in a group at first; when full grown they are green with yellow stripes. Larvae may take up to four years to complete growth. Dark brown pupa protected by loosely woven silk cocoon just below soil surface. May spend more than one winter as a pupa.

Adult 52-70 mm. Wings brown, black and white, with transparent areas; body brown and black.

Adult 80-115 mm. Forewings brown, white and black; hind wings pink and black. Body pink, black and grey.

Privet hawk-moth *Sphinx ligustri*
Range Resident in much of Europe but excluding Scotland. Some moths migrate from south to north Europe each year.
Habitats Gardens, parks and chalk downs.
Habits Flies at night in June and July, and is attracted to light and to flowers. Eggs are laid singly on leaves of privet or, less often, lilac and ash. Black droppings are useful clue to presence of larvae. Pupa brown, formed in chamber in soil; may remain there for two winters.

Larva Green, striped with white and purple; tail-end horn black and yellow.

Death's-head hawk-moth *Acherontia atropos*
Range Resident in Africa and Middle East but each year migrates northwards to Europe, including Britain.
Habitats Attracted to light at night but more likely to be met with as larva in vegetable gardens and farmland.
Habits Arrives in N. Europe from May to September; commonest in late summer. Eggs are laid singly, usually on leaves of potato, woody nightshade and deadly nightshade. Larva either yellow and green or yellow and brown, with purple stripe on each side and yellow horn at rear; brown form feeds at night, others by day or night. Pupa glossy brown, formed in chamber below soil surface. Does not overwinter in Europe.

Adult 102-140 mm. Black and brown wings and body, with yellow skull marking on thorax. Produces sound.

Humming-bird hawk-moth *Macroglossum stellatarum*
Range Resident in S. Europe; regular migrant to N. Europe.
Habitats Occurs wherever there are flowers; often attracted to jasmine.
Habits Reaches N. Europe in July and August. Flies by day; hovers like humming-bird and produces high-pitched buzzing sound. Eggs are laid singly, usually on bedstraws but sometimes on wild madder. Pupa brown, on ground near foodplant.

Adult 38-50 mm. Forewings brown, hind wings orange and brown. Body brown, with black and white patches. Feeds in flight.

Larva Green and reddish-brown, with white spots and lines; yellow line on sides. Horn blue and yellow.

Pine hawk-moth *Hyloicus pinastri*
Range Much of Europe, including Britain and Scandanavia.
Habitats Coniferous woodlands, especially those of pine and spruce.
Habits Appears between June and August, flying at night and attracted to light and to honeysuckle flowers. Groups of two or three eggs are laid on pine or spruce needles. Young larva green with white stripes along body – difficult to see; later becomes ringed with black, white and red, and has a black and brown horn. Pupa brown, formed in chamber under ground. Becoming more common as coniferous forests increase in number.

Adult 75-90 mm. Dark and light grey wings and body. Well camouflaged on bark.

Oak hook-tip *Drepana binaria*
Range Most of C. and S. Europe, including S. Scandinavia and S. Britain.
Habitats Oak woodlands.
Habits Appears in May and again in July and early August in two broods. Flies at night. Larva feeds on oak leaves; tail end of body lacks claspers as do other species of hook-tip family. Nearly black pupa, which overwinters, is hidden inside silk cocoon between two leaves or in rolled leaf of foodplant.

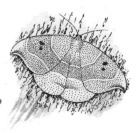

Larva Usually green, with bluish- and yellowish-brown markings. Holds tail upwards.

Adult 22-38 mm. Yellowish-brown or grey-brown wings and body; female usually paler than male.

Adult 32-38 mm. Brown body and hind wings; forewings brown, with black-edged pink and white markings.

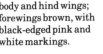

Peach-blossom *Thyatira batis*
Range Throughout Europe but less common in north.
Habitats Woodland with undergrowth of brambles, in large gardens and in parks.
Habits Flies at night in June and July; sometimes with second flight in August and September. Moth is named after blossom-like markings on forewings. Small batches of eggs are laid on edges of bramble or raspberry leaves. Larva pale red-brown, with darker lines along body; feeds only at night. Keeps tail raised. Pupa brown or dark red, protected inside silk cocoon attached to leaf of foodplant. Autumn pupae overwinter.

Magpie moth *Abraxas grossulariata*
Range Most of Europe, including far north.
Habitats Gardens, waste ground, hedgerows and scrubland.
Habits On the wing at night from early June to early September. Will fly by day if disturbed. Eggs are laid singly or in small batches under leaves of garden gooseberry and currant bushes, hawthorn, blackthorn, heather and heaths. Larva overwinters in spun leaf of foodplant or nearby. Pupa black and yellow, in transparent cocoon on foodplant or in nearby crevice.

Adult 35-43 mm. White, orange and black body and wings. Varies individually in pattern and much used in genetical studies.

Larva A 'looper'. Colours similar to those of adult. Usually feeds in a small group. Distasteful to most birds.

Adult 25-28 mm. Male's wings greyish-brown and brownish-white. Body brown and black. Female similar but with only tiny wing; flightless.

Winter moth *Operophtera brumata*
Range C. and N. Europe. Common in most of Britain.
Habitats Orchards, woods, gardens and hedgerows.
Habits Fully winged night-flying males and spider-like females emerge from pupae between October and December. Female climbs up trunk of tree or shrub to lay single egg or small batches of eggs on buds or twigs of apple, pear, other fruit trees, hawthorn, rhododendron, oak and other woodland trees. Sticky bands round trunk of garden fruit trees are used to trap ascending female moths. Striped green 'looper' larva hatches in late April or May and spins light web over developing leaves and flowers, sometimes tunnelling into buds. Larva lowers itself to ground on silk thread in June and pupates there.

Swallow-tailed moth *Ourapteryx sambucaria*
Range Throughout Europe except for N. Scotland
and N. Scandinavia.
Habitats Gardens, edges of woods, parks and
hedgerows.
Habits Flies at night in July and August; often seen
resting by day under ivy leaves. Eggs are laid on ivy,
privet, blackthorn, hawthorn or other trees and
shrubs. Larva overwinters partly grown among
branches of foodplant. Pupa brown and black, in
cocoon suspended horizontally by both ends on
foodplant.

Adult 42-54 mm. Wings
and body light yellow,
with yellowish-brown
markings. One of few
tailed European moths.

Larva Brown, with
darker lines. A 'looper'
when moving.
Deceptively twig-like
when at rest.

Adult 45-52 mm. Wings
and body white and
brownish-black, or
nearly entirely black.

Peppered moth *Biston betularia*
Range Most of Europe, including Britain and
Scandinavia.
Habitats Woodlands, orchards, parks and gardens.
Habits Flies at night, usually from May to July, but
may have two broods in warm years and fly again in
August and September. Eggs are laid on leaves of
almost any deciduous tree and on bramble and rose.
Larva green or brown, very twig-like; moves in
looping motion; feeds at night. Adult moth
demonstrates how moths in industrial areas may
evolve black forms that match sooty backgrounds.
Green or brown pupa overwinters in chamber below
soil surface.

Puss moth *Cerura vinula*
Range Commonest in S. Europe but occurs in most of Europe.
Habitats Found wherever there are trees, but prefers poplars.
Habits Flies at night between May and July. Eggs are laid in batches of two or three on shoots and young leaves of poplar, sallows, ash and birch. Larva whirls around tail filaments to ward off parasitic wasps, mantids and other small enemies. Pupa brown, hidden inside tough cocoon of silk and chewed wood placed flat against tree trunk, not far from ground; may overwinter twice.

Adult 60-82 mm. Body yellow, grey and black. Forewings grey and white; hind wings white in male, grey in female. Abdomen grey.

Larva Cat-like viewed from front. Body green, white and purple. Rears up if provoked and everts filaments.

Adult 50-64 mm. Body yellowish-brown, forewings black and brown with buff tip, hind wings whitish. At rest resembles broken twig.

Buff-tip *Phalera bucephala*
Range Much of Europe, including Scotland and Scandinavia.
Habitats Woodlands, gardens and parks.
Habits Flies at night in May and June; sometimes also in July and August. Egg batches are laid on leaves of various trees. Hairy, yellow and grey larvae feed in groups. Pupa formed under ground; may overwinter twice.

Lobster moth *Stauropus fagi*
Range C. and S. Europe, as far north as S. England and S. Scandinavia.
Habitats Moist woodlands; especially downland beechwoods in England.
Habits Flies at night from May to July; sometimes also in August. Small batches of eggs laid on leaves of various trees. Larva has scorpion- or lobster-like reaction when disturbed. Pupa overwinters in cocoon on ground.

Adult 56-70 mm. Brown and white body and wings; bark-like.

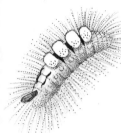

Pale tussock *Dasychira pudibunda*
Range N. and C. Europe, but absent from Scotland.
Habitats Woodlands, gardens, hedgerows and hop-fields.
Habits On the wing, at night, in May and June. Eggs are laid in batches on branches and twigs of oak, birch, elm, other deciduous trees and on hops. Hairy pupa overwinters inside frail cocoon on or near ground.

Larva Green and white, or yellow and green. Has four white toothbrush tufts, and at tail end a long hair-pencil.

Adult 42-64 mm. Wings and body greyish-white, grey and brown. Always rests with forelegs extended forwards.

Adult 32-45 mm. Wings and body mostly white, but tail-tuft usually dark brown.

Brown-tail moth *Euproctis chrysorrhoea*
Range Most of Europe, including C. and S. England.
Habitats Old hedgerows, orchards, wasteland, and roadside trees.
Habits Flies at night during July and August. Eggs are laid in batches on twigs of hawthorn, fruit trees and other shrubs and trees, and are covered by female with irritant tail-tuft scales. Larvae spin large communal silken web, but they leave the web to feed. Larval hairs are irritant. Dark brown pupa formed inside silk cocoon attached to foodplant.

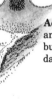

Garden tiger *Arctia caja*
Range Common throughout Europe.
Habitats In gardens and wherever there are low-growing plants.
Habits Flies during July and August, mostly at night. At rest will display hind wings and produce sound if disturbed. Eggs are laid in batches under leaves of various plants. Larva overwinters when small until about June. Pupa dark brown, formed on ground in silken cocoon. Moth and larva poisonous to insect-eating birds.

Adult 50-80 mm. Forewings brown and white; hind wings orange-red and blue-black. Body red and black.

Larva The 'woolly bear'. Brown, with small white spots; hairs black on back, red-brown on sides.

Adult 34-45 mm. Forewings grey-brown, with greenish sheen, marked with red. Hind wings red. Body black.

Cinnabar *Tyria jacobaeae*
Range Most of Europe. In Scotland confined to coasts.
Habitats Wasteland, pastures, meadows and sand dunes.
Habits Appears between May and July. Flies mainly at night. Eggs laid in batches under leaves of ragwort or, less often, on groundsel. Larvae black and orange-yellow; usually feed in small groups, often by day; distasteful to most birds.

Silver-Y *Plusia gamma*
Range Migrant to C. and N. Europe from south of
Alps.
Habitats Farmlands, gardens, meadows and
wasteland.
Habits Flies either by day or night, often attracted to
honeysuckle and other flowers but seldom settles.
Eggs are laid on clover, thistle and other plants,
including lettuce, peas and other crops. Pupa dark
brown, inside silk cocoon under leaf of foodplant or
among dead leaves on ground. Never overwinters in
N. Europe.

Adult 35-40 mm. Wings
and body brown and
grey, with shiny silvery
'Y' mark on forewings
and with tufts of scales
on thorax.

Larva Green with white
and dark green stripes.
Larva overwinters in S.
Europe.

Turnip moth *Agrotis segetum*
Range All of Europe except for N. Scandinavia.
Habitats Arable farmland, wasteland and gardens.
Habits Flies at night from May to July, with rare
second-brood flight in autumn. Larvae, which
overwinter, cut down plants at ground level or feed
underground on roots and tubers. Pupa formed in soil
and silk chamber.

Adult 31-44 mm.
Brownish-grey and
yellowish-brown
forewings and body,
nearly white hind wings.

Adult 35-40 mm. Pale
grey and black
forewings and body;
hind wings mostly
white.

Grey dagger *Acronicta psi*
Range Lowlands of most of Europe.
Habitats Hedgerows, open woodlands, orchards,
parks and gardens.
Habits May have two broods, but normally has only
one flight, in June. flies at night. Larva hairy, blue-
black, with yellow line along back and black-edged
red spots on sides; feeds alone on leaves of various
trees and shrubs. Pupa formed in cocoon in bark
crevice; overwinters.

Gardens can be one of the most productive places for the butterfly watcher. The closeness of your garden to open countryside will affect the number of species you are likely to see, but gardens with the right sort of flowers can attract several kinds of butterflies and moths even in the centre of large cities. In a large garden you may even be able to provide foodplants for larvae.

Buddleia (*Buddleja davidii*), a perennial shrub, could be one of the first things to plant, preferably in autumn. Butterflies like the Small Tortoiseshell, Peacock, Comma and Red Admiral will be attracted to its summer blooms during the day and several species of moths at dusk and in the evening. Lavender (*Lavandula* species) and pink-flowered varieties of ice-plant (*Sedum spectabile*) could be the next things to plant, and also aubretia (*Aubretia deltoidea*) if you have a rock garden. You should also try and find room for red valerian (*Centranthus ruber*), chinese aster (*Callistephus sinensis*), sweet william (*Dianthus barbatus*) and tobacco plant (*Nicotiana*). For a large wild garden you can now buy wild-flower seeds: common honeysuckle (*Lonicera periclymenum*), bird's-foot trefoil (*Lotus corniculatus*), the larval foodplant of many blues and burnets, and lady's smock or cuckoo flower (*Cardamine pratensis*), the foodplant of larval Orange-tip butterflies. Never take plants from the countryside for your garden; you will be breaking the law if you do so.

Having attracted butterflies and moths to your garden, you can find out which species visit particular plants, at which time of day and year they arrive, the numbers of specimens, how long they feed, and so learn a lot more about their biology. Remarkably little detail has been published about the habits of most of our common butterflies and moths so there is a good opportunity for some original detective work.

A shorthand notebook is a good buy for recording your observations. All records should include a note of the place, date and time; weather conditions (temperature, wind, sunshine, humidity); and, at night, whether the moon is up or not. You will find that the closer you look the more there is to discover. Adding your records to those of a national or county survey may be possible – your local natural history society or County Trust should be able to advise you.

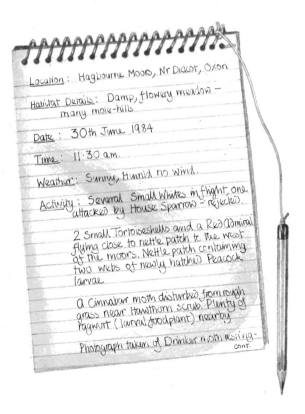

Location : Hagbourne Moors, Nr Didcot, Oxon

Habitat Details : Damp, flowery meadow – many mole-hills

Date : 30th June 1984

Time : 11·30 a.m.

Weather : Sunny, Humid no wind.

Activity : Several Small Whites in flight, one attacked by House Sparrow – rejected.

2 Small Tortoiseshells and a Red Admiral flying close to nettle patch to the west of the moors. Nettle patch containing two webs of newly hatched Peacock larvae

a Cinnabar moth disturbed from rough grass near Hawthorn scrub. Plenty of Ragwort (larval foodplant) nearby

Photograph taken of Drinker moth resting –

cont.

Many species can be bred through from egg or larva to adult if you can provide a regular supply of the usual foodplant or a known alternative. This is one of the easiest ways of studying the life-history of a butterfly or moth.

One of the simplest breeding cages you can make comprises a cylindrical tube made from flexible transparent plastic, held in place by an empty tin can at the base and wire mesh or nylon netting at the top. Alternatively, you can make a wooden cage with a removable glass front. Many small larvae can be kept in a ready-made transparent plastic sandwich box lined at the base with blotting paper to soak up condensation. Leaves remain fresh for at least a day in such a box.

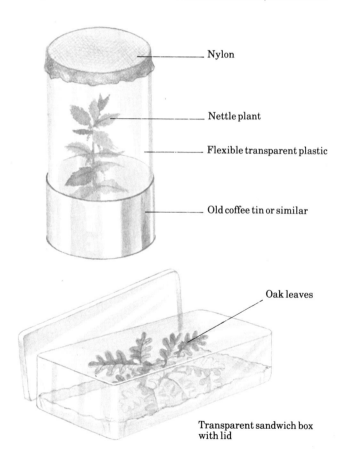

Nylon

Nettle plant

Flexible transparent plastic

Old coffee tin or similar

Oak leaves

Transparent sandwich box with lid

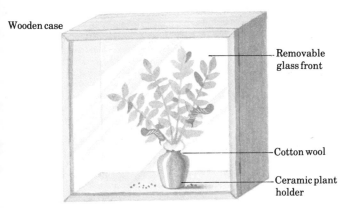

Wooden case

Removable glass front

Cotton wool

Ceramic plant holder

If you are lucky enough to find the eggs of a butterfly or moth, cut off the part of the twig or shoot and put it in a sealable plastic bag. As soon as you get home, place the cut end of the cutting in water in a sturdy jar. Pack cotton-wool around the stem so that emerging larvae cannot fall into the water.

Larvae are easier to find and can be dislodged from a bush or tree by giving the branch a sharp jolt, or they can be looked for on low-growing plants. Look out for such evidence of larval activity as leaf damage, curled leaves, silk strands and webs and droppings. Collect a few larvae at a time and always make a note of the foodplant. You can also buy eggs and pupae from dealers.

As a moth or butterfly farmer you should remember to handle larvae as little as possible and to use a soft brush rather than your fingers when moving them. Keep only one species in each breeding cage, do not overcrowd your cages and keep the cages dry and out of direct sunlight. It is also important to clean the cages daily and to renew the food supply.

A few larvae, like those of Orange-tips are likely to eat one another, so to be really safe keep only one specimen in each container except for recognized gregarious species.

After one or two weeks most larvae will change into pupae unless they have been attacked by parasitic wasps or flies. However, some species overwinter as larvae. Most butterfly larvae pupate attached to a twig, branch or leaf of the foodplant, so stand some twigs in the cages. Many moth larvae pupate in the soil, so for these you should provide a container of slightly moist peat. Twigs are useful for both moths and butterflies because emerging adults need something on which to cling while their wings expand and dry. Overwintering larvae or pupae should be placed outdoors in a plastic box in an unheated building.

The nettle-feeding larvae of the Peacock and Small Tortoiseshell are good species to start with. If you are successful in rearing out butterflies, try and release them as soon as possible, one or two at a time, generally in the area where you collected the eggs or larvae.

It is difficult to identify some adult butterflies and most moths without taking them home for comparison with illustrations in detailed field guides. You may also need to collect and keep specimens for reference when doing biological studies.

The equipment you will need for collecting includes a canvas knapsack, a shorthand notebook, a pencil and ball-point pen, a net, pill-boxes, a plastic box for larvae and a 1:25000 map of your area. Specialist items such as pill boxes, killing jars and setting equipment (see below) are obtainable from entomological suppliers (see your local Yellow Pages).

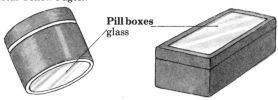

Pill boxes
glass

Collecting butterflies can start as early as April, when overwintering species like the Brimstone and Small Tortoiseshell are on the wing on warm sunny days. During most of the summer, especially in July, you will soon get to know most of your local butterflies and will probably need to capture only a few specimens. When wielding a net make quick sideways sweeps forehand or backhand and then flick the end of the net over the frame to trap your butterfly. Black kite-nets are probably the easiest to use.

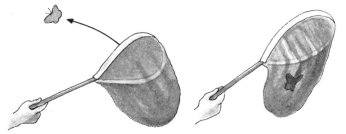

Day-flying moths should be caught and transferred to glass-bottomed pill-boxes for identification. Moths are more difficult to identify than butterflies and seldom come to rest where you can see them clearly. Night-flying moths are best collected using a white sheet and a mercury-vapour lamp fixed above it. Moths will be attracted to the light and most of them will settle on the sheet and can be captured in pill-boxes. Moon-less, warm, humid nights are the best for moths.

Sugaring is usually a less successful but a fascinating method of attracting night-flying moths. With a 2.5 cm wide paint brush smear a boiled-up mixture of black treacle or cane sugar, rotten bananas, apples and a dash of amyl acetate

Catching moths at night   rope   **Sugaring posts**

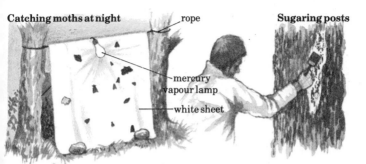

mercury
vapour lamp

white sheet

(obtainable from a chemist), and perhaps a little beer or brown rum, in 30 cm-wide vertical bands on each of a row of fence posts near woodlands and pay regular visits during the night.

When garden flowers are in bloom examine these from dusk onwards for nectar-seeking moths.

You may have to kill some moths and 'set' them before you can identify them accurately. Killing jars usually consist of screw-topped jars that have an absorbent layer of plaster of Paris or blotting paper at the bottom. Pour into the jar a little ethyl acetate (again from a chemist), pop in your specimen and leave it there for at least an hour. Setting, the mounting of a killed specimen on a flat board, is a skilled job, but is not difficult to learn. Make sure that the size of special pins you use is right for your storage boxes. You will also need forceps, setting-pins and paper strips as well as setting-boards. Leave the moths on the boards for at least three weeks in a warm dry atmosphere away from beetles and other pests and label each specimen with the place, time and date of capture.

Finally remember to record in your notebook data such as type of habitat and weather conditions, as well as the standard pin-label date (see page 73).

Setting specimens

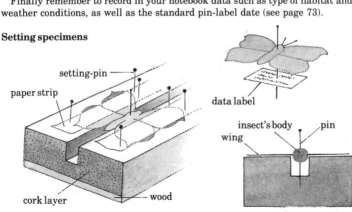

setting-pin

paper strip

data label

insect's body   pin

wing

cork layer   wood

Some species of butterfly and moth are restricted to particular areas of Britain although the larval foodplant is widely distributed; examples are the northern Scotch Argus butterfly and Scotch Annulet moth, and in the south the Marsh and Heath Fritillaries and the Jersey Tiger. Other species, like the woodland specialists, have a wider geographical distribution but are nearly always restricted to special vegetational zones.

To be sure of seeing a good selection of butterflies it is difficult to beat the chalk grassland hills of south-eastern England, especially where there are a few clumps of trees and a stretch of mature hedgerow. You could expect to see Chalk-hill Blues here and possibly an Adonis Blue and a Silver-spotted Skipper, as well as butterflies that occur in both chalky and non-chalky places such as the Meadow Brown, Small Heath and Common Blue. The North and South Downs and the Chiltern Hills are places you should visit.

Also good for butterflies are sandy heaths, usually with heather (*Calluna*), heaths (*Erica*) and gorse. Good heaths still exist in the New Forest in southern England, Skipworth Common in Yorkshire and in a few other places, but sadly many heaths are being ploughed up for farming. Typical heathland butterflies are the Silver-spotted Blue, the Green Hairstreak and the Grayling.

The moorlands of Scotland and northern England (plus Dartmoor and Exmoor) are also good places for butterflies, and for many moths (e.g. Emperor, Fox and Northern Eggar) whose larvae feed on moorland heaths and heathers.

Do not neglect special habitats like sand dunes, where you are likely to find Common Blues and Cinnabar moths among others. Salt marshes (e.g. around Chichester, Sussex and the Thames estuary) and areas of shingle (Dungeness and parts of Norfolk, for example) have a distinctive moth fauna.

Wasteland in and around towns is often the home of a surprisingly large number of species. Buddleia plants, a garden escape, are often present and attract several species of butterflies and moths, like the Peacock and Silver-Y, and also the Wall butterfly whose larvae feed on grasses, which are always present in wasteland.

Most localities are worth investigating, even seemingly unpromising places, if you want to put your nature detective work to the test.

Amateur Entomologist's Society, 4 Step Close, Orpington, Kent, BR6 6DS

British Butterfly Conservation Society, Tudor House, Quorn, Loughborough, LE12 8AD

Dal, B., 1982, *The butterflies of northern Europe* (Croom Helm)

Carter, D. J., 1979, *Observer's book of caterpillars* (Warne)

Carter, D. J., 1982, *Butterflies and moths in Britain and Europe* (Pan)

Fitter, R. & A. and Blamey, M., 1974, *The wild flowers of Britain and northern Europe* (Collins)

Ford, E. B., 1977, *Butterflies* (Collins)

Higgins, L. G., & Riley, N., 1980, *Field guide to the butterflies of Britain and Europe* (Collins)

Martin, W. Keble, 1982, *The new concise British flora* (Michael Joseph & Ebury)

Rothschild, M., & Farrell, C., 1983, *The Butterfly gardener* (Michael Joseph)

South, R., 1973, *Moths of the British Isles* (Warne) [2 vols]

Watson, A., 1981, *Butterflies* (Ward Lock) [N. Europe]

Whalley, P. E. S., 1980, *Butterfly watching* (Severn House)

Your local library will probably be able to help you with the addresses of your local Natural History society and County Naturalist Trust.